I0762657

HYPERLOOP

Joanne Mattern

CREATING YOUNG NONFICTION READERS

Little Mitchie books spark curiosity and support early nonfiction reading for students in Grades 2-3. Designed to build vocabulary, support second language learners, and prepare readers for middle-grade content, each book includes helpful tips for parents and educators to build confidence and deepen understanding of the world.

TIPS FOR READING NONFICTION WITH BEGINNING READERS

Talk about Nonfiction

Begin by explaining that nonfiction books give us information that is true. The book will be organized around a specific topic or idea, and we may learn new facts through reading.

Look at the Parts

Most nonfiction books have helpful features. Our *Little Mitchie* titles include color photographs and graphic aids, a table of contents, a glossary, and an index. Share the purpose of these features with your reader.

Color Photos and Graphic Aids

A lot of information can be found by "reading" photos, charts, maps, and other graphic aids found within nonfiction texts. Help your reader learn more about the different ways information can be displayed.

Table of Contents

Located at the front of the book, this list shows the big ideas within the text and the page numbers where they can be found.

Glossary

Located at the back of the book, the glossary defines key words and phrases that are related to the topic. These words and phrases can be found in the text in colored type.

Index

Located at the back of the book, an index is an alphabetical list of topics and the page numbers where they can be found.

With a little help and guidance about reading nonfiction, you can feel good about introducing a young reader to the world of *Little Mitchie* nonfiction books.

Little Mitchie is an imprint of:

2001 SW 31st Avenue
Hallandale, FL 33009
mitchelllanepub.com

First Edition, 2027.

Author: Joanne Mattern
Designer: Bobbie Houser
Editor: Tricia Hoffman

Library of Congress Cataloging-in-Publication Data
Title: Hyperloop / by Joanne Mattern

Description: Hallandale, FL :
Mitchell Lane Publishers, [2027]

Identifiers:
ISBN 979-8-89260-869-5 (library bound)
ISBN 979-8-89260-966-1 (eBook)

Library of Congress Control Number: 2026936107

PHOTO CREDITS
Alamy: Malp, 5; Jim West, 15; Malp, 17; Photononstop, 18; Dreamstime: Spyrakot, 6; Siiptok, 8; Shutterstock: petrmalinak, Cover, 1; Volodimir Zozulinskyi, 11; Sundry Photography, 13; Markus Mainka, 19; petrmalinak, 20; Stoqliq, 22.

TABLE OF CONTENTS

Chapter One

MOVING FAST!

Evan's family was traveling on a new kind of train. It was called the Hyperloop.

"Hyperloop is the fastest way to travel on land," his father said.

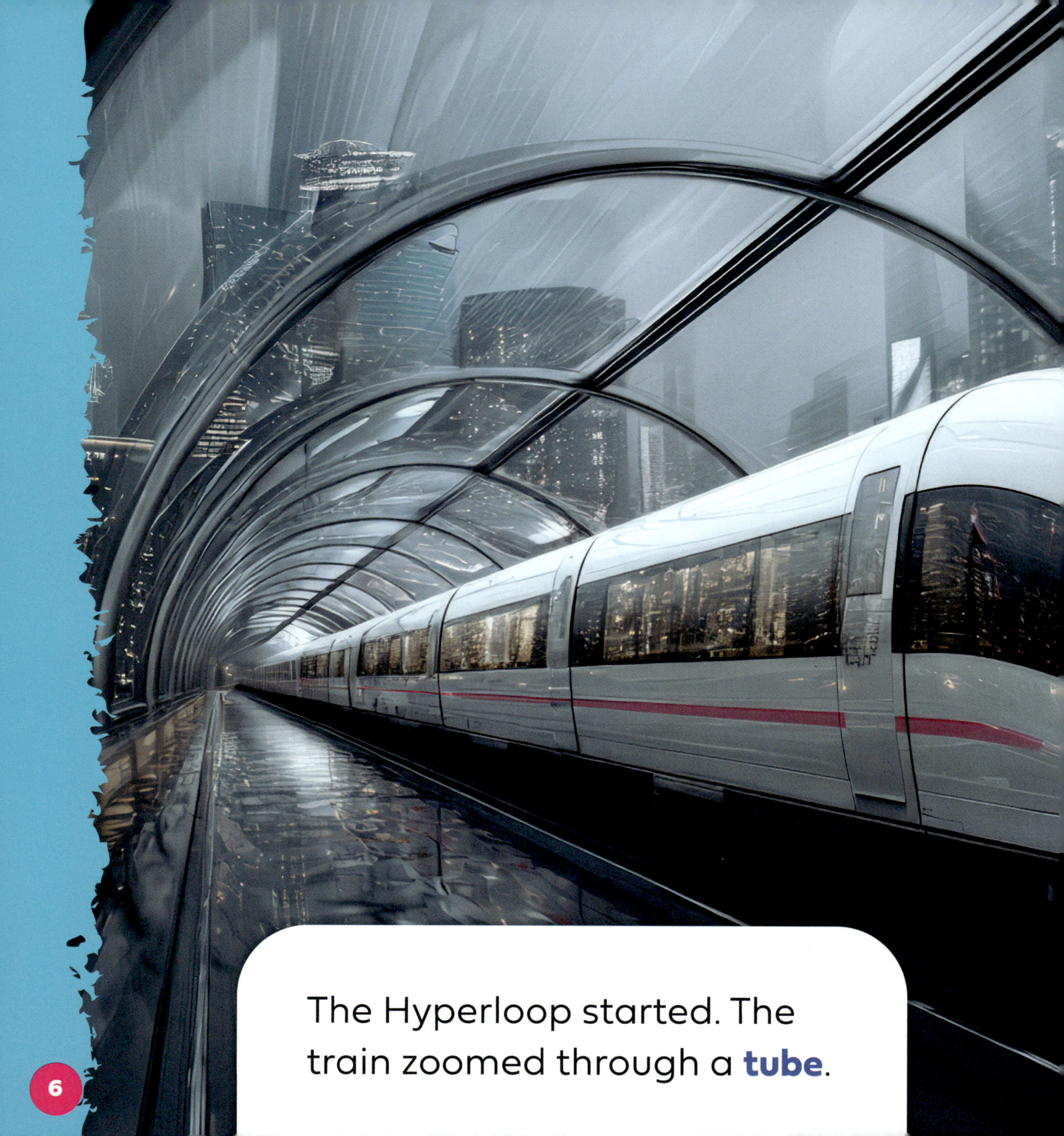

The Hyperloop started. The train zoomed through a **tube**.

"It feels like we are floating on air," Evan said.

"We are," said Evan's mother. "That is how the train can move so fast."

After 20 minutes, Evan's father said they had gone more than 200 miles (322 kilometers)! That was much faster than riding in a car.

"Someday, Hyperloop systems will carry people all over the world," Evan's father said.

Chapter Two

HYPERLOOP TODAY

Most trains run on wheels. Wheels rub the rails, which causes **friction** and slows the train down.

In 2013, Elon Musk wrote a paper about his idea for the Hyperloop. It would not run on wheels. Instead, the Hyperloop would float on a layer of air. This would cut down on friction and let it go faster than a traditional train.

Several companies started building Hyperloop systems. These trains run in long tubes. Machines suck almost all the air out of the tubes to create a near-**vacuum**. There is little air to push against the train and slow it down.

GIVE KIDS A CHANCE
Elon Musk held a series of student contests to get ideas for how to build a Hyperloop.

In 2016, Virgin Hyperloop built a **test track** in Las Vegas. Four years later, two passengers rode on the Hyperloop for the first time. The train zoomed along at 107 miles (172 kilometers) per hour.

A TEAM EFFORT

Companies in other countries built test tracks too. Lots of people want to make Hyperloop happen!

Chapter Three

THE FUTURE OF HYPERLOOP

Hyperloop faces many problems. The biggest one is the price tag. Building tubes to connect cities would be very **expensive**. It would cost billions of dollars!

Hyperloop systems would also need a lot of land to build on. It would take a lot of time and money to get enough land.

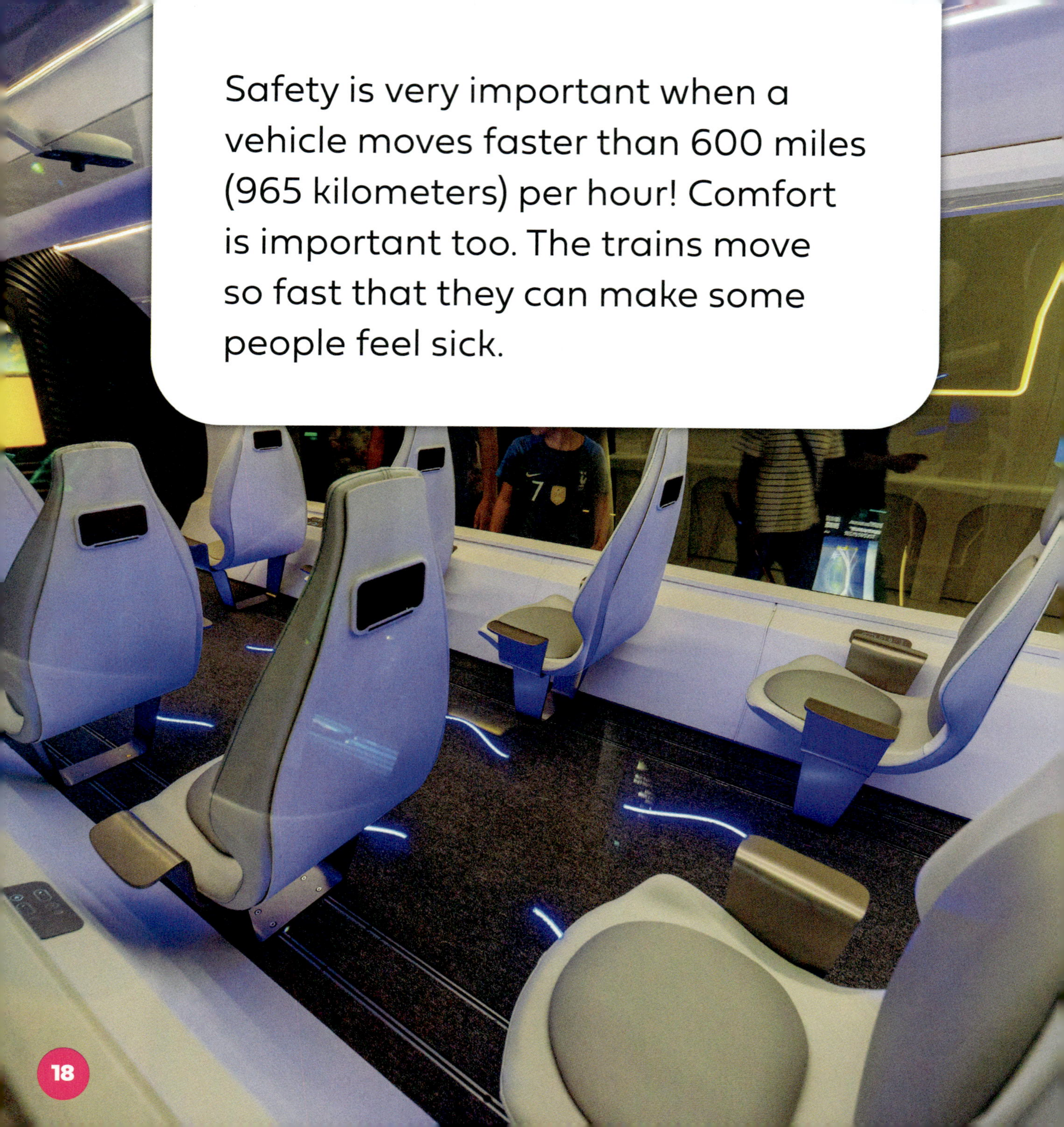

Safety is very important when a vehicle moves faster than 600 miles (965 kilometers) per hour! Comfort is important too. The trains move so fast that they can make some people feel sick.

OTHER FAST TRAINS

China already has some super-fast trains. These trains use magnets to move.

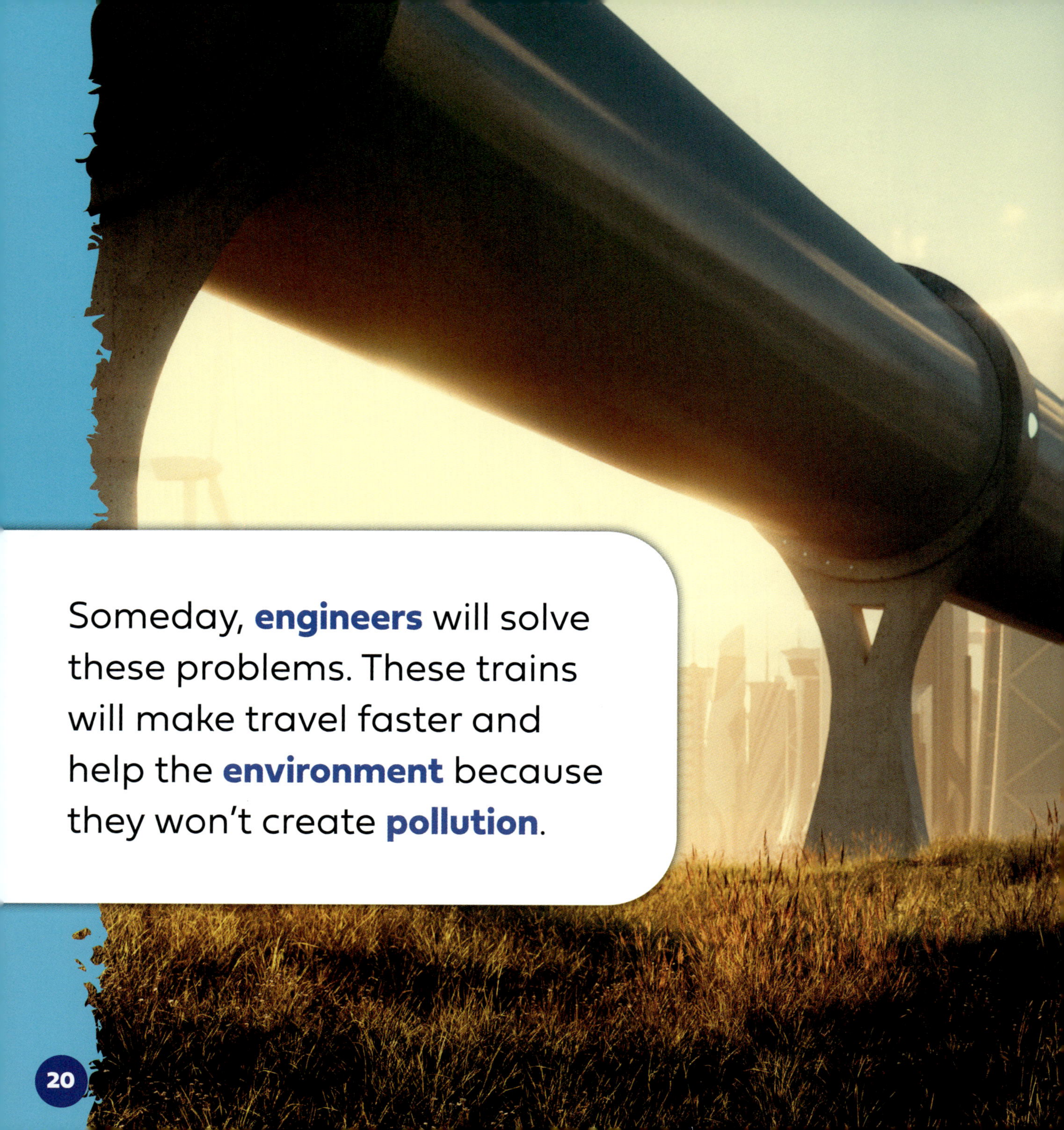

Someday, **engineers** will solve these problems. These trains will make travel faster and help the **environment** because they won't create **pollution**.

FREE FOR ALL

Elon Musk made his Hyperloop ideas available to everyone. That will help companies work together to build these super-fast systems.

The future of Hyperloop could make the world a faster, cleaner, and more fun place!

LET'S LOOK AT A HYPERLOOP

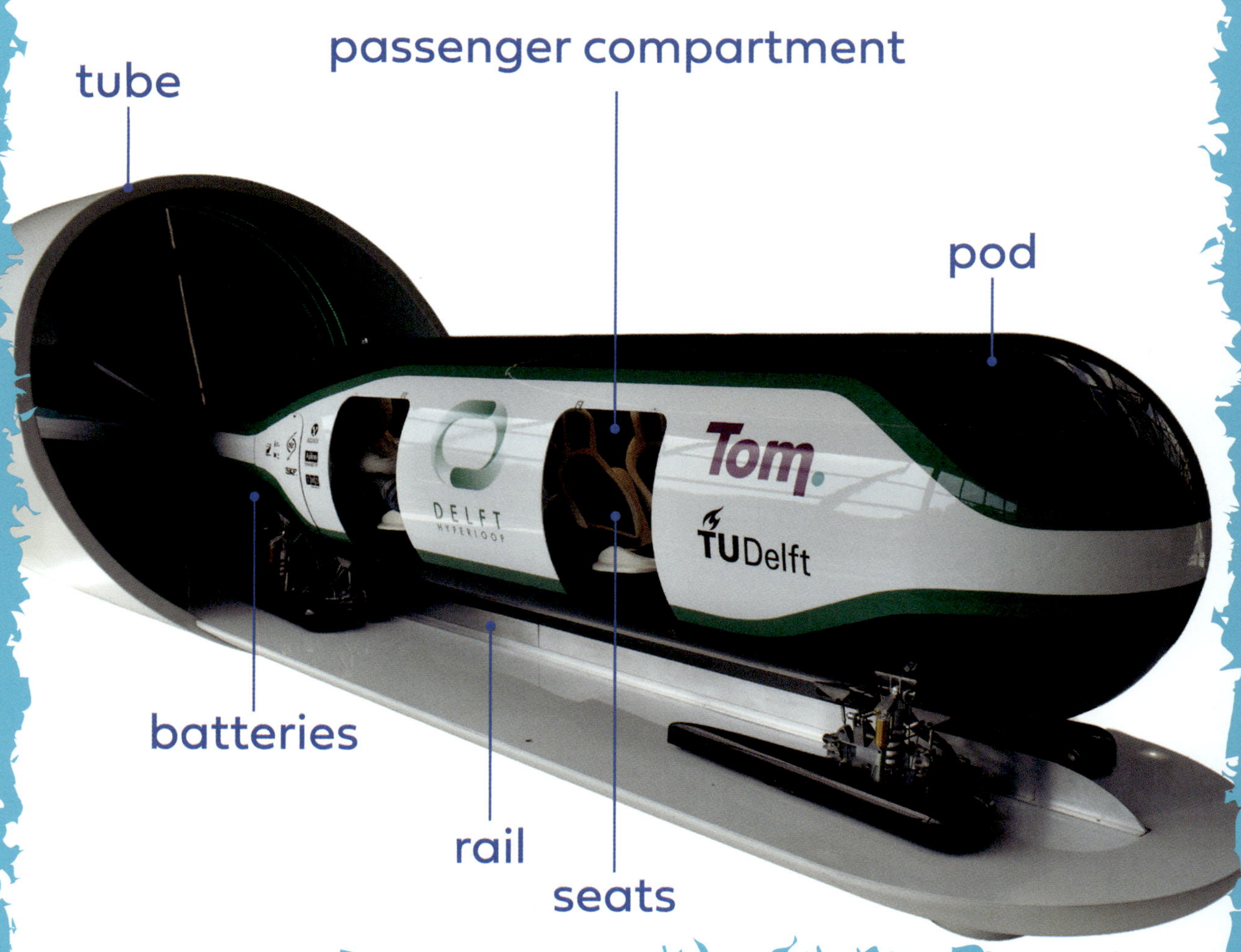

GLOSSARY

engineers (en-juh-neerz) people who are trained to design and build machines

environment (en-vye-ruhn-muhnt) all the living and nonliving things around us, such as plants, animals, air, and water

expensive (ik-spen-siv) costing a lot of money

friction (frik-shuhn) the force that slows down objects when they rub against each other

pollution (puh-loo-shuhn) harmful things that damage the air, land, or water

test track (test trak) a place where new vehicles are tested

tube (toob) a long, hollow cylinder

vacuum (vak-yoom) a sealed space from which all air has been removed

FURTHER READING

Gleisner, Jenna Lee. *High-Speed Trains.* Jump!, Inc., 2020.

Klepeis, Alicia. *Superfast Trains.* Jump!, Inc., 2022.

ON THE INTERNET

Hyperloop Facts for Kids
https://kids.kiddle.co/Hyperloop
The article explains how Hyperloop systems work—and the good and bad things about them.

Shanghai Maglev Train Facts for Kids
https://kids.kiddle.co/Shanghai_maglev_train
Explore the fastest train in the world and how it works!

INDEX